Read
the Bible
at the Eucharist

by
Michael Vasey
Tutor of Cranmer Hall, St. John's College, Durham

GROVE BOOKS LIMITED
Bramcote   Nottingham   NG9 3DS

CONTENTS

PREFACE

Some of the ideas in this booklet first saw light of day as a short contribution at the Society of Liturgical Study Conference on 'Word and Liturgy' held in Oxford in September 1984. My thanks are due to the Group for the Renewal of Worship for its encouragement, to loyal friends for their support and prayers, and to God for his mercy and grace.

Michael Vasey

THE COVER PICTURE

is by Peter Ashton

First Impression January 1986

ISSN 0144–1728
ISBN 0 85174 018 X

1. PREAMBLE

'Attend to the public reading of scripture, to preaching, to teaching' wrote St. Paul to Timothy in a letter dealing with the ordering of the life and worship of the church of Ephesus (1 Tim. 4.13). This booklet deliberately limits itself to the first of these[1] and its aim is to stimulate those responsible for worship to think again about the place of the reading of scripture in the ordinary weekly gathering of the church. It is not an attempt to produce a perfect blue-print suitable for every parish situation, but to introduce readers to some of the discussions afoot in the wider church and to identify some helpful questions for assessing local practice. It is a companion to *Intercessions in Worship*[2] which tried to do the same for the prayers, and had in mind particularly sections 20 and 21 of Rite A of the ASB.

While the rubrics of the ASB provide a bewildering flexibility for the prayers, the opposite seems to be the case with the reading of scripture. The lectionary adopted for use with the ASB, first approved in 1978, makes provision on a two-year cycle for every Sunday communion. The sole lawful flexibility it allows seems to be the omission of the 'epistle' or Old Testament reading when this is not nominated as the 'controlling lesson (see Note 2, p.281 ASB). The only other lawful Sunday communion lectionary is that of the Book of Common Prayer, supplemented in 1965 and 1980, and also published in a convenient form each year by SPCK-Mowbrays. In November 1984 General Synod heavily defeated a move to allow the use of the Roman Catholic Sunday lectionary as an alternative. Where a church's main morning service is sometimes morning prayer instead of a eucharist there are four lawful alternatives to the ASB provision: the inaccessible lectionaries of 1871 and 1922, the 1961/80 lectionary, and the ASB provisions for Holy Communion (see Note 3, p.281 ASB).

Although the ASB encourages flexibility with the prayers and virtually forbids it in the reading of scripture, practice on the ground seems to follow similar patterns in both cases. Some parishes follow the ASB lectionary, though often in a wooden and formal way that gives the hearers little sense of the human context and force of the set passages. Other churches ignore the lectionary, either because it does not fit their monthly pattern of services or their teaching programme, or because the other things they wish to do on a Sunday morning make its provision seem excessively long. Some virtually abandon the public reading of scripture altogether, save a few verses to introduce the sermon.

It is probably rare for the Bible readings to be the focus of great expectancy on the part of the worshippers. They are often overshadowed for many by the sermon and the communion. Frequently they function as a sort of 'mental cigarette' between hymns or songs—a breather until we

---

[1] For a parallel examination of preaching in a eucharistic context see Ian Bunting's *Preaching at Communion* (Grove Worship Series nos. 78, 79).
[2] Grove Worship Series no. 77 by Michael Vasey.

can respond again! At best they are seen as a useful way of encouraging lay participation, a fairly safe way of adding to the number of folk up front without doing too much harm. The wise preacher probably assumes that the congregation has not listened too attentively to the readings; over-optimism at this point means he or she has lost many of the audience before they start.

Amongst preachers opinion about the ASB lectionary seems fairly sharply divided. Many appreciate its thoughtful attempt to represent the broad outline of biblical theology. Many preachers find its apparent thematic structure simultaneously irritating and alluring, and hanker to preach on passages it does not use.

These different responses have a variety of causes. Producing and assessing lectionaries is a complex, not to say obstruse, activity. The principles of a lectionary, or the arguments for adopting one at all, have not been discussed widely in the modern church. Nor, indeed, has the rationale of reading scripture at all in worship; its virtual omission from most 'informal' worship indicates how weak conviction is here. These issues will receive some consideration in the course of this booklet. However there are other factors and assumptions at work and it may help to make clear some of those which influence the approach here taken.[1]

Some assumptions:
. . . 1. Worship is an activity of the church
It is an expression of a common life in, and a relationship with, Jesus Christ. The life and prayer of the individual Christian exists in dialogue with that of the church, learning from, shaped by and contributing to the corporate prayer. This means, amongst other things, that the form of worship is a matter for the church. Worship is formed, under God, within the life of the church. It has some God-given fixed elements (of which the public reading of scripture is one), but its form is created within the Christian community using elements from the Christian past and from contemporary life. PCCs, incumbents, Synods seek to regulate and shape something they neither own nor create.[2]

Two things flow from this assumption. One is that Christian worship is properly the subject of corporate decision-making. It is open to argument at what level of church life a decision properly belongs, and whether a particular decision has wrongly assessed local need. There may be good reason for dispensing with a particular rule or provision in some circumstances[3], but there must be at least a presumption in favour of the corporate decision. The second is:

. . . 2. Respect for corporate patterns
Church life is full of patterns, customs, traditions, practices that are part

[1] Also explored in *Intercessions in Worship, op. cit.*
[2] cf. *Anglican Worship Today* pp.38-43.
[3] 'And so ecclesiastical law should be interpreted charitably provided that nothing is done contrary to the Gospel and the Apostles', Ivo of Chartres, quoted in R. C. Mortimer *Western Canon Law* (A. & C. Black, 1953). But note Aidan Kavanagh, 'In our day it seems to require more courage to obey a rubric or law than to break it'! (*On Liturgical Theology*, p.102).

of the way Christians participate in worship. These include service times, hymn tunes, choruses, liturgical responses, expected patterns of prayer. These often need changing, enriching, challenging, even creating, but they cannot be simply ignored or bypassed without destroying the corporate nature of worship and making the majority mere spectators (whether angry, bored or content!). Taking these seriously affects the pace of church life and the tasks of liturgical leadership.[1] Congregations need to have present and new patterns articulated if they are to cope with change. They need clear patterns if they are not to be humiliated by clerical whim—but this does not mean only one pattern per church; three or four different patterns can be internalized and used where appropriate.

. . . 3. Tensions and Balance

Patterns of worship need to accommodate many of the tensions and balances of Christian life. Often success here is the mark of good liturgy. Examples of such balances are: crucifixion and resurrection; individual and corporate; Jewish and Gentile(i.e. insider and outsider); historical continuity and eschatological newness. Two other tensions are those between local and universal and between primary and wider Christian fellowship. The first refers to the tension between membership of this congregation and the universal church. The second refers to the often more painful tension between the movement in which I found life (evangelical, charismatic, catholic etc.) and the wider life of my part of the church universal (e.g. the Church of England). The new Anglican forms are in part an attempt to hold these latter balances:

. . . 4. Understanding the structure of Rite A.

Rite A is probably best seen as an anthology of prayers and readings to be used in a fixed framework. The basic framework is a three-part meeting. Part 1: Hearing and receiving the word of God. Part 2: Prayers and Thanksgivings. Part 3: Eucharist. This framework is being adopted by many Christian bodies worldwide as a self-conscious return to the pattern that emerged in the second century (see next chapter). It is possible to dismiss this as a sort of 'patristic fundamentalism', but to do so is hardly fair; the desire is to overcome divisions between (and within) denominations by rediscovering common roots. However there is a danger that a past pattern will be adopted without understanding its purpose or examining whether it is effective today.

'Hearing and receiving the word of God' is, then, the congregation's task in the first part of Rite A. Hearing and responding to the word of God is part of all biblical worship. It is possible to take too simple a view of when hearings and responding take place, to see the readings and sermon as the hearing, and other elements such as songs as response. However we often hear God's word in the singing (compare Col. 3.16 and Ps. 95.7b ff.) and reading and preaching are often a form of response. 'Receiving the word' is an active process expressed in many ways; to this we shall return.

[1] *Intercessions in Worship,* p.15ff.

. . . 5. A lost art.

For a variety of reasons most modern people do not have the skills to take part easily in a gathering the size of a local congregation.[1] Steps need to be taken to help both individuals and congregations in this. In the part of worship we are considering this means not only the arts of public reading and speaking, but also the skills of responding by posture and verbal response.

Assessment

How does one evaluate worship? Any gathering of God's people is unique and mysterious because it is the encounter of God with his people. The consequences of worship are hidden and incalculable. God meets us in our folly as well as in our Spirit-inspired hope. Aidan Kavanagh rightly speaks of 'a certain *violence*' being involved in it.[2] At the same time it is possible to ask what purpose God has for his people in worship and at least attempt some answer.

Vatican II's *Constitution on the Sacred Liturgy,* in a famous sentence, states that 'the liturgy is the summit toward which the activity of the church is directed; it is also the fount from which all her power flows.' (section 10). Summit and source; focus and fount. This statement suggests two questions that one might ask of any worship event: 1. Does it embody or express this congregation's relationship with God? 2. Does it feed the life and mission of this congregation? If asked of the readings at the eucharist, the answer to 1. is usually 'in a wooden and symbolic way', and to 2. is 'No'! If people leave church unchanged by the reading of scripture, it does not say much for the way the Bible reading expressed their relationship with God!

What sort of change should we expect worship to achieve? Ian Bunting warns of the pressures towards an exclusive emphasis on building up the church and preparing for the eucharistic action.

> 'Too strong an attachment to the task of building the church may lead to a cosy, shallow, or triumphalist, style of preaching.'[3]
> 'Such rich notes in the service can, however, easily waylay the congregation into pride, and complacency, and an overconfidence which does scant justice either to the seriousness of sin or to the partial fulfilment of the kingdom of God in this world. The difficulty for the preacher arises from the pressures exerted upon him by the shortage of time . . . and by the hidden imperatives to say something which enhances the victorious themes of the Great Thanksgiving . . . Certainly one has no room to stand back, to question, to reflect, to engage in the kind of open-ended dialogue which is all part and parcel of the *theologia crucis.*'[4]

The same pressures are at work in the choice of readings. It is our understanding of the eucharistic context, and not scripture itself, that has encouraged this easy optimism.

[1] cf note 2 on p.4 above; also *Intercessions in Worship* pp.10, 17.

[2] *ibid.* p.94 cf 'It follows a law of change even unto death rather than the stately laws of organic evolution . . . The worshipping assembly is neither a machine nor a species of plant.'

[3] *Preaching at Communion (i), op. cit.,* p.7.

[4] *ibid.* p.8.

2. PAST

Jewish background

'And he came to Nazareth, where he had been brought up; and he went to synagogue, as a his custom was, on the sabbath day. And he stood up to read; and there was given to him the scroll of the prophet Isaiah.' (Luke 4.16, 17)

The public reading of scripture was an integral part of normal worship for the devout Jew as he met at the synagogue week by week (cf. Acts 13.15, 15.21, 2 Cor. 3.15). It is this familiar liturgical act that St. Luke sets at the start of his account of Jesus' ministry. An increasingly outraged congregation grasps that this 'local boy' is applying the text to himself and this movement; his response is to remind them of a whole string of Old Testament stories that they must often have heard read.

This incident, so often quoted by modern Christians, points up the importance of scripture and its public reading to the Jews of Jesus's time. Although conflict often centred on how scripture was fulfilled, the importance Jesus gave to scripture and the place it had in his life and teaching cannot be denied (cf. John 5.39-47, Luke 24.25-27).

Written scriptures were part of biblical religion from the first, although their precise relation to the rest of Israel's religious life is disputed and seems to have varied.[1] Before the invention of printing, radio or television books (and scrolls) necessarily fulfilled a different role in a community. Much communication was oral and public. A primary function of books was to preserve and witness what was said (cf. Exod. 24.4, 7, Is. 8.16, Jer. 36) and to communicate at a distance (cf. Jer. 29). Letters were often intended to be read aloud in public. Although literacy was widespread (cf. Judges 8.14) responsibility for copying and teaching what was written rested with recognized and respected figures in society (cf. scribes[2] and priests—Hos. 4.6, Mal. 2.7). The written word and its public recitation were an indispensable part of social and public life. But this did not mean that private reading was not also important—Psalm 119 is ample evidence for this, and for the fact that the Psalter is a literary, not a liturgical, collection.[3] Through the course of God's dealing with Israel the growing written embodiment of his revelation naturally assumed increasing importance. This is illustrated in Ezra's solemn reading of the law (Neh. 8.1-8) and in the development of the synagogue where Jews gathered to read, study and pray.[4]

Israel celebrated and remembered its relationship with God in many ways, informal and liturgical; prominent among these were prayers, songs and public and domestic festivals. The public reading of scripture served to keep the community's grasp of God's revelation alive, full and pure. It had a part in all the levels of Israel's religious life. The law was

---

[1] G. Fohrer *Introduction to the Old Testament* (SPCK, 1976) pp.37ff; *Cambridge History of the Bible* vol. 1, p.30ff. 'Books in the Ancient World'.
[2] M. D. Goulder *Midrash and Lection in Matthew* (SPCK, 1974) pp.10ff.
[3] cf. G. Fohrer *op. cit.*, p.295, 'a wisdom book for theological edification'.
[4] H. H. Rowley *Worship in Ancient Israel* ch. 7.

read in the temple on the Day of Atonement.[1] Scripture was read at home.[2] Public reading formed the centre of synagogue gatherings.

The detail of what system was followed in the reading of scripture in the synagogue is the subject of very lively scholarly debate. [3] It seems that the following can be said with certainty:

1. Two lectionaries developed separately, a festal lectionary and a sabbath lectionary. The motive for the first was the reading of passages appropriate to the festival; the motive for the second was that the whole of God's primary revelation (the *Torah*, i.e. Pentateuch) should be heard by the people.

2. Although local custom varied in detail the continuous reading *(lectio continua)* of the Pentateuch sabbath by sabbath developed early. The Pentateuch was read over a period of about three years. This reading, in Hebrew, was followed by a traditional Aramaic translation *(Targum)*.

3. There was also a reading from the prophets. At the time of Jesus this was probably not fixed.[4] After this someone might be invited to give an address.

Responsibility for directing the synagogue's worship rested with the 'ruler of the synagogue'. Any competent Jew might be asked to read. The sabbath portions of the Pentateuch were quite long and were customarily read by more than one person. At other services during the week part of the sabbath portion of the Pentateuch would be read.

Early Church

The first Christians inherited from Jesus and the apostles similar attitudes and expectations about written scriptures. St. Paul, for all his clarity about the 'weakness' of the law and the powerlessness and opaqueness of any written text without the Holy Spirit (Rom. 8.3 cf. 2 Cor. 3.6), speaks warmly of 'the oracles of God' (Rom. 3.2) and of the advantages accruing to Timothy from a life-long exposure to scripture (2 Tim. 3.15). Love of the Old Testament shines through the New Testament writings as does the high level of biblical knowledge assumed in their hearers.

This attitude to written scripture extends to the New Testament writings themselves. Already within the New Testament canon they are referred to as scripture (2 Pet. 3.16). St Paul expected his letters to be read publicly to the churches and to be taken with great seriousness (1 Thess. 5.27; 2 Thess. 3.14; Col. 4.16; 2 Cor. 10.10, 11). The book of Revelation

---

[1] Mishnah Yoma 7.1, Sotah 7.7ff., cf. Deut. 31.10-13.
[2] See R. T. Beckwith 'The Daily and Weekly Worship of the Primitive Church in relation to its Jewish Antecedents' in *The Evangelical Quarterly* Vol LVI (1984) pp.78-80.
[3] Usefully summarized in Goulder, particularly p.173ff. (I don't endorse his views on the origin and purpose of the Gospel!). See also R. T. Beckwith and note his reference to the article by J. Heinemann.
[4] Again, see R. T. Beckwith.

warns in traditional terms against tampering with the given text (21.18, 19). Austin Farrer, in his fine chapter on biblical inspiration, writes, 'We have to remember that the business of writing about sacred matters was viewed by the Jew with a solemnity we cannot easily recover . . . that they were writing books of the *nature* of sacred scripture, they did not doubt'.[1]

The early Christians were part of a church on the move and their style differed in many ways from their first Jewish context. They appear to have been well ahead of their time in using the convenient papyrus book (codex) and parchment notebook forms as opposed to the more traditional but cumbersome scroll. Their motives appear to have been practical and reflect a serious commitment to teaching converts. C. H. Roberts writes that 'the earliest [Christian] manuscripts were the product not of the book trade but of communities whose members included businessmen and minor officials well used to writing . . . On the rapid circulation of literature among the churches and on its regular and public reading much of the coherence of the early Church must have depended'.[2] While he can speak of 'a prejudice in favour of the direct oral tradition' he can write, 'Christian culture and education were bookish through and through; reliance on the book, initially a legacy from Judaism, was soon a weapon of the Church in its fight against paganism'.[3] It is important to add quickly a reminder that books were instruments in a public community life. Public reading was an essential part of this.

Our first description of a Christian eucharist outside the New Testament is in Justin Martyr (c. A.D. 150):
> 'On the day called Sun-day an assembly is held in one place of all who live in town or country, and the records of the apostles or writings of the prophets are read for as long as time allows. Then when the reader has finished the president in a discourse admonishes and exhorts us to imitate these good things. Then we all stand up together and offer prayers; . . .'[4]

It includes the three-part structure for the church gathering to which reference has been made and which has been adopted as the model in contemporary reform of worship. It is worth asking why it emerged.[5] A fuller description in Hippolytus' *Apostolic Tradition* (c. A.D. 215) makes it clear that catechumens (who had been enrolled and were under instruction) were allowed to be present for the first part, and were then dismissed before the prayers and eucharist. The emergence of a common form is most reasonably explained as an intuitive act witnessing to the unity of the scattered churches (cf. 1 Cor. 11.2, 14.33b-36). There seem to me to be two reasons why the reading and exhortation came first, one practical and one theological. Practically it allowed the unbaptized to be present and exposed to the scriptures. Theologically it embodied the fact

[1] *Glass of Vision* (Dacre Press, 1948) p.54.
[2] *Cambridge History of the Bible* vol. 1, pp.63, 64.
[3] *Ibid.* pp.61, 66.
[4] R. C. D. Jasper and G. J. Cuming (ed.) *The Prayers of the Eucharist* (Collins 1975) p.19.
[5] cf. my brief discussion in *Intercessions in Worship*.

that it was and is the message from God, centred in Jesus Christ, that draws together and creates the church.[1]

In Justin's account it seems clear that no lectionary was followed. As much scripture was read as was practical and quite probably the reading began before everyone had gathered. Later accounts usually give three readings, Old Testament, New Testament and Gospel. In fourth century Antiochene tradition four readings came from the law, the prophets, the apostolic writings (a much more sensible term than our 'epistle' or 'New Testament reading') and the Gospel. This is reminiscent of synagogue practice and is evidence that a symbolic significance was seen in the order in which different parts of scripture were read. By contrast with the synagogue the most significant were read last.

There is evidence that approximately fixed readings developed early, primarily associated with festivals. In the time before Constantine two annual festivals dominated the church's year, the Christian Passover and the Christian Pentecost. Baptisms were mainly celebrated in the former. A preparatory period of prayer and instruction reached its climax on the Saturday when the church gathered to fast and pray with those to be baptized. Through the night 'they shall be read to and instructed'.[2] The series of readings would naturally reflect the links between the Passover, baptism and Jesus' death and resurrection. St. John Chrysostom speaks of the reading of Acts between Easter and Pentecost as traditional and provides evidence that Genesis was normally read in Lent.

It would be impossible to look in detail at the emergence of the traditional lectionaries but it is worth highlighting some points:
1. Particular readings and books were associated with Christian festivals. These increased and expanded as the circumstances of the church changed after the conversion of Constantine. A particular development of this time was the emergence of Christmas and Epiphany. Lent and Advent grew as part of the great festivals to come.
2. For ordinary Sundays the principle of *lectio continua* was used, a book was selected at local discretion and read until it was finished. Preaching often followed a similar pattern, as some of the great collections of patristic sermons show.
3. Under pressure of length and time readings tended to be abbreviated and Old Testament readings dropped.
4. Readings were read directly from the Bible. Starting and finishing points were indicated in the margins or in separate lists. Only later were separate books of readings produced; our oldest is from the eighth century. Medieval lectionaries followed the pattern of other liturgical books of the time and included only the part needed by the particular minister.

---

[1] Compare the comment of Howard Hageman on later Protestantism's fascination with over-extended prayers of invocation., '. . . the impression left . . . that of a congregation trying to make sure that God would be present before it wasted its time with the rest of the business.' (*Celebrating the Word* (Anglican Book Centre, Toronto, 1977) p.57).

[2] G. J. Cuming (ed.) *Hippolytus: A text for Students* (Grove Liturgical Study 8, 1976) p.18.

5. Each reading tended to be followed by a prayer, song or response to allow people to receive what they had heard. Often the Psalms were used.

6. Vigils, such as the one referred to at Easter, were an important occasion for hearing scripture. Early Christians often prayed in the middle of the night (remember there was no electricity); the night was seen as an important time for reciting psalms and hearing scripture. In the monastic office pattern the bulk of scripture reading occurred during the night office.

Justin's account mentions 'the reader' and it seems that this soon emerged as a particular ministry or office in the church, presumably because of the skills required and because the task was recognized as important. Readers were at first responsible for all the lessons and this continued beyond the time of Cyprian after which the gospel came to be reserved to the deacon.[1] in the fourth centuries readers were often young boys whom bishops and priests took into their homes to instruct and train in the Christian faith.[2] Athanasius was such a young reader; Augustine is an example of a bishop who followed this practice. It provides evidence of children playing a prominent part in worship although in a firmly educational context.

Two quotations from Augustine's sermons give a lively sense of how the reading was regarded by people and preacher:
> 'When the gospel was being read, you paid great attention. As the story unfolded before you it took shape before the eyes of your heart. You saw, not with your body, but with your mind how our Lord Jesus Christ sat at table in the Pharisee's house. You saw too how a woman, renowned in the city as a sinner, gatecrashed her way in . . .'

> 'I had prepared myself for a homily on a short psalm, and told the cantor which it was. But he seems to have got a little confused, and in fact he sang a different psalm for you. But in this seeming mistake I see the will of God, and so I have made up my mind to follow it, rather than the one I originally had in mind.'[3]

Reformation and after
Cranmer's Preface to his Prayer Books[4] gives a vivid sense of the way the reading of scripture (even in Latin) had been overshadowed in medieval times 'by planting in uncertain Stories, and Legends, with multitude of Responds, Verses, vain Repetitions, Commemorations, and Synodals' Restoring public knowledge of scripture was a major part of his programme as the placing of Bibles in every church in 1538 made clear.

The main instrument chosen by Cranmer for this purpose was his revised form of Morning and Evening Prayer. He placed at the heart of these services two readings, one from the Old and one from the New Testament.

[1] J. G. Davies *Journal of Ecclesiastical History* vol. 14 (1963), p.13.
[2] *Roles in the Liturgical Assembly* (tr. M. J. O'Connell) (Puelblo, NY 1981), pp.198 and 223 (notes 31-34).
[3] Quoted in John N. M. Wijngaards *Reading God's Word to Others* (Mayhew-McCrimmon, 1981).
[4] In 1662 this is entitled 'Concerning the Service of the Church'.

This brilliantly embodied the complementary nature of the two parts of scripture in a way that has been profoundly formative among Anglican Christians. Cranmer's lectionary for these services followed the civil rather than the ecclesiastical year, and arranged that the Old and New Testaments should be read through consecutively, usually a chapter at each service. The psalms were to be read through each month. He appointed special lessons, often only for the New Testament reading, for most major festivals on red-letter saints days.

His assumptions were that clergy, and at least some laity, would use these services every day, and that Holy Communion on Sundays would be preceded by Morning Prayer with its readings. For this reason he viewed the epistle and Gospel as additional readings and was content to follow the tradition of the Sarum rite fairly closely. His aims were simple, clear and commendable. However his reforms ignored a number of the principles which are virtually inherent in the church's reading of scripture at the eucharist. The subsequent complex history of the reform of Anglican lectionaries from 1559 to 1978 can be seen as the progressive correction of Cranmer's work. 1559 saw the introduction of special lessons for every Sunday. 1871 and 1922 recognized that church life cannot be ruled by the civil year but has to be responsive to the major Christian festivals. The 1872 'Shortened Services Act' allowed the Communion service to be celebrated without Morning Prayer; finally in 1965 the implications of this were recognized with the provision of Old Testament readings to go with Cranmer's epistles and Gospels. The result of this progressive reform is the rationalized lectionary authorized in 1980 and published annually by SPCK-Mowbrays 'According to the Book of Common Prayer supplemented by the Additional Alternative Lectionary'.

One other echo of the post-reformation era is perhaps worth a mention, namely the controversy between Hooker and some Puritans over whether there was any benefit to be gained from the mere reading of scripture apart from sermons. These Puritans asserted that only sermons, indeed only good sermons that were themselves not read, were effective in awakening faith. The idea is still around in evangelical circles! Hooker, in his lengthy reply, notes the apostles' use of the written word, quotes scriptural examples that attribute greater power or seriousness to the read word[1], and disputes Puritan exegesis that limits preaching to sermons.[2] Hooker by no means denies 'the especial advantages which sermons naturally have to procure attention'.[3] In the overvaluing of sermons he sees a danger that 'they make the price and estimation of Scripture otherwise notified to fall'[4], and drive some to despair who cannot get to hear good preaching[5]:

> 'Surely if we perish it is not the lack of scribes and learned expositors that can be our just excuse. The word which saveth our souls is near us; we need for knowledge but to read and live.'[6]

[1] *Laws of Ecclesiastical Polity* Bk. 5. XXII.4 (2 Chron. 34.18-21; Deut. 31.11-13; Lk. 16.31).

[2] *Ibid.* XXII.9 on 1 Cor. 1.21 'the Apostle . . . must needs by "the foolishness of preaching" mean the doctrine of Christ'.

[3] *Ibid.* XXII.20.

[4] *Ibid.* XXII.7.

[5] *Ibid.* XXII.17

[6] *Ibid.* XXII.15 alluding to Rev. 1.3.

3. PRESENT

The aim of this chapter is to map out briefly some of the schemes and approaches relevant to Anglican life today. Assessment and evaluation will take place in the next chapter.

ASB

The calendar and two-year lectionary of the ASB represent a new approach within the Church of England to the reading of scripture at Communion. Adopted in 1979, they owe their general form to proposals put forward in 1967 by the Joint Liturgical Group (JLG), a British ecumenical team of liturgists. The members of this group include Baptists and Roman Catholics and it has exercised a creative influence in the renewal of worship. Established in 1963, it saw part of its task as: 'The planning of a Calendar, Forms of Daily Service, and a Lectionary which the churches might be glad to have in common.'[1]

Basic to the reform of the lectionary has been a reshaping of the Christian year, designed to take seriously the rhythm of parochial life and to give a coherent theological shape to the year. The traditional seasons of Advent and Lent start later than the natural 'terms' of church life. Major festivals on weekdays are largely ignored. JLG therefore proposed a simple pattern in which the nine Sundays before Christmas would unfold 'the movement from creation to incarnation' in which the Old Testament passage would be the required and controlling reading; between Christmas and Pentecost the controlling reading would be the Gospel and the period would explore the birth, ministry, death and resurrection of Jesus; after Pentecost the controlling reading would be the new Testament reading and the season would focus on Christian life in the Spirit.

In outline the ASB adopts this approach, although some of the more radical aspects of JLG's proposals were not accepted, such as the abandonment of the Epiphany and Ascension Day and of the traditional names of Lent and Advent. Particularly controversial has been the influence of the Sunday themes, hidden away on page 1092 of the ASB but asserting their influence through thematic collects and opening and post-communion sentences. The original JLG report makes clear that the passages of scripture were chosen first and not the themes: '. . . recognition is given to the fact that all Scripture is not of equal significance, that there are certain passages of special significance, and that in order to represent the wholeness of witness a balance of selection must be observed.' 'In the post-pentecost period, the biblical passages were *first* selected, bearing in mind the general thrust of the season, and only then were they ordered and given sequence so that some general progression of theme emerged.'[2]

The complementary readings for Morning and Evening Prayer on Sundays and weekdays also owe their inspiration to the JLG. The House of Bishops vetoed a proposed daily eucharistic lectionary so that a version of the Roman Catholic daily eucharistic lectionary was adopted. This latter, of course, needed adaptation to fit the ASB Calendar—as the rules on page 1071 indicate.

[1] R. C. D. Jasper (ed.), *The Calendar and Lectionary* (Oxford, 1967) p.ix.
[2] *Ibid.* p.19.

Roman Catholic Three-Year Lectionary

'The treasures of the Bible are to be opened up more lavishly so that a richer fare may be provided for the faithful at the table of God's word'[1]. With these words the Second Vatican Council commissioned a new lectionary that appeared in 1969, with a second edition and extended Introduction in 1981. This latter represents a thorough and theologically careful exploration of the place of scripture in the liturgy.[2]

In comparison with the ASB the three-year cycle allows more scripture to be read, although both inevitably make significant omissions. Three readings are appointed for every Sunday; the provision is generally slightly shorter than that of the ASB. The Roman Catholic lectionary makes a sharp distinction between festival seasons and what it calls 'Ordinary Time' so that the Sundays between Epiphany and Lent and between Trinity and Advent follow the provision for Ordinary Time. In Ordinary Time the decision was made 'not to have an organic harmony of themes designed to aid homiletic instruction. Such an arrangement would be in conflict with the genuine conception of liturgical celebration. The liturgy is always the celebration of the mystery of Christ . . .'[3] In Ordinary Time the Gospels and Epistles are read 'semi-continuously' and Old Testament passages are to correspond with the Gospel. So Matthew, for example, is read in Year A. Ancient tradition is followed in reading Acts and John semi-continuously in the Easter season.

In practice the link between Gospel and Old Testament reading, combined no doubt with traditional expectations, means that the homily is usually based on the Gospel, and the Epistles are ignored. Another weakness often remarked on is a tendency to omit verses within a reading. This is also an irritating feature of the Roman Catholic daily eucharistic lectionary adopted in the ASB. Unlike the lectionaries of the ASB there are no alternatives given for the Apocrypha.

An Anglican coming to this (or any other Roman Catholic liturgical provision) is astonished by the developed and subtle framework of church law within which it operates.[4] The danger that a legalistic attitude should dominate over pastoral concern is recognized:

> 'Pastors of souls must therefore realise that, when the liturgy is celebrated, more is required than the mere observance of laws governing valid and lawful celebration. It is their duty to ensure that the faithful take part knowingly, actively and fruitfully.'[5]

It would be easy to mock at the canonical learning and legal subtlety sometimes exercised by Roman Catholic liturgists in justifying pastoral common sense. However Anglicans may have something to learn in terms of learning a theological and pastoral approach to the rules of church life that has more to it than 'I follow the rules I like'! Section 82 of the Introduction allows more discretion in the handling of weekday lections than any Church of England provision.[6]

[1] *Constitution on the Sacred Liturgy* section 51.

[2] *Lectionary for Mass: Introduction* (Office of Publishing Services, United States Catholic Conference, 1312 Massachusetts Ave. N.W., Washington D.C. 20005).

[3] *Ibid.* section 68.

[4] Cf. e.g., Kevin Seasoltz *New Liturgy, New Laws* (Liturgical Press, Minnesota, 1980).

[5] *Constitution on the Sacred Liturgy* section 11.

[6] 'The one using the Order of Readings for weekdays must check to see whether one reading or another from the same biblical book will have to be omitted because of some celebration occurring during the week. With the plan of readings for the entire week in mind, the priest in that case arranges to omit the less significant selections or suitably combines them with other readings, if they contribute to an integral view of a particular theme.'

Three further features of the Roman Catholic provision deserve a mention. One is the revival of responsorial psalm singing as a way of responding to the reading. A second is the careful concern for presentation of readings and the promotion of acclamations, responses, antiphons, gestures, posture and silence 'to promote active participation' by the people. A third is the revival of the ministry of lector or reader and a giving of appropriate training for what is seen as a spiritual ministry.

As noted earlier a proposal to allow the Roman Catholic lectionary to be a legal alternative in the Church of England on an experimental basis was thrown out of General Synod in November 1984 after powerful speeches by Colin Buchanan. Miss Christian Howard and the Archbishop of York. The main arguments advanced were the absence of connection between the readings, the benefits of having the ASB readings printed out in one book, and a dislike of liturgical 'fidgets'.[1] An important factor was affection for the ASB provision as a 'home-grown' common lectionary.

Common Lectionary
Despite this firm rejection and the decision of General Synod to extend the authorization of the ASB, the Church of England is likely to find itself under continuing pressure to adopt something like the Roman Catholic lectionary. The recent Standing Committee Report *The Worship of the Church* (GS 698) envisages the production of a supplement to the ASB (section 41) as well 'a thorough and sustained evaluation of the ASB 1980' (section 43). The 1978 Lambeth Conference passed a resolution:

'The Conference recommends a common lectionary for the Eucharist and the Offices as a unifying factor within our Communion and ecumenically; and draws attention to the experience of those Provinces which have adopted the three year Eucharistic Lectionary of the Roman Catholic Church.'

The reference is to North America where many denominations including Anglicans have experimented with versions of the Roman Catholic lectionary:

'In countless towns, villages and urban parish neighbourhoods groups of clergy and laity, Catholic, Anglican and Protestant, are meeting each week to work exegetically and pastorally with the readings of the approaching Sunday.'[2]

In some cases there has been more than a decade of experiment, and a revision of the lectionary has now been issued for consideration in the churches. The most significant change is in the treatment of the Old Testament where Black American churches and others protested at the suppression of narrative and at a tendency 'to reduce the Hebrew revelation to a matter of little consequence apart from the fact of Jesus Christ'. The new proposal adopts a semi-continuous treatment for much of Ordinary Time:[3]

Year A (Matthew)—20 Sundays of Pentateuchal material (Abraham's call to Moses' death); 3 Sundays of Ruth; 3 of prophetic eschatology

Year B (Mark)—14 of Davidic narrative; 4 of Wisdom literature

Year C (Luke)—10 of the Elijah-Elisha cycle; 15 of Major and Minor prophets.

[1] *Proceedings of General Synod* vol. 15.3, p.1059ff.
[2] *Common Lectionary: The Lectionary Proposed by the Consultation on Common Texts* (The Church Hymnal Corporation, 1983).
[3] *Ibid.* pp.21-22.

4. A SECOND LOOK

It is easy for liturgical proposals and practices to gain great authority, particularly if they appear to have some basis in church history and if they fit in with familiar patterns of church life. It is important to ask hard questions of emerging new patterns; they may improve on present practice without achieving all that is possible or providing what the future church needs.

Why we read the Bible in worship

There are clearly a number of different reasons for reading the Bible in worship and it is important to identify them and explore their implications.

First, by reading scripture the church acknowledges its relationship to God the Holy Trinity, to Jesus Christ and to the apostolic message. It is an act of faith, of gratitude and of submission. It expresses the fact that the church is created by the proclamation of the Gospel and is summoned to attend to the voice of its Lord.

Second, it expresses too the church's relationship to the pivotal acts of God in history. Our life is inextricably bound up with the historical figure of Jesus, a Jew, who lived at a certain time in history. His life, teaching, death and resurrection are decisive for us. Not only that but our life is part of God's dealings with one historical people; God is the God of Abraham, Isaac and Jacob.

Third, the public reading of scripture gives physical expression to the church's acceptance of the Bible as the 'oracles of God', intended by him not only for its original audience but also for us 'upon whom the end of the ages has come' (1 Cor. 10.11; Rom. 15.4). It is an acknowledgement that the message and teaching of Jesus found decisive and authoritative expression in apostolic teaching, teaching inspired by the Holy Spirit and set out for us in these 'sacred writings'.

These first three reasons are essentially *symbolic.* They are ritual acts of considerable potency which embody convictions that need expression within the corporate Christian life and cannot really find embodiment in any other way. The fact that they are symbolic needs to be weighed carefully in our loose-textured culture in which church life is often shaped by private and literate people unsympathetic to much symbolic action. With these first three reasons for the public reading of scripture it is almost more important that the reading is done and heard with appropriate seriousness than that it is understood.

That the public reading of scripture has a symbolic side to it has many implications worth exploring. Ritual and symbol are different from teaching and explanation; they need some element of repetition and rely on meanings embodied in actions. The custom of three readings at communion in the usual order embodies (and therefore teaches) theological truths about God's revelation and about the way the parts of scripture belong together. Reading the Gospel last embodies the centrality of Jesus Christ in the Christian understanding of scripture. It also illustrates well how symbolic actions can go wrong if they are not handled and taught with understanding; many worshippers pick up from this a distorted theology that puts 'our Lord's teaching' above his death and resurrection and the apostolic gospel.

The symbolic aspect of reading scripture has an implication for the style of this part of worship, and this needs to affect both presentation and congregational attitude. Discovering this style is an important task for a local congregation. It should not simply imitate royal or military ceremonial or sensible committee procedure ('propose that we take the minutes as read'!). It must flow from the Christian Gospel itself: joy, faith, humanity, reverence, glory.

Also this symbolic dimension needs to find embodiment in the furniture and action that provide the context for the reading. For many people, as noted earlier, this means learning new social skills and being helped and encouraged through their initial embarrassment. Appropriate and familiar responses have their part here; compare the response in the new New Zealand Anglican eucharist:

'Here what the Spirit is saying to the church.
Thanks be to God.'

Standing for the reading of the Gospel expresses the centrality of Christ to scripture and the faith that he speaks in his word; it can claim some basis in scripture (Neh. 8.5), although in other cultures another posture may be more appropriate.[1] Turning to face the reader increases involvement. In churches where congregations follow the readings in their own books there is often awkwardness at this point; learning to turn to the reader, to look up for responses, and to sing them, can help. The more extended sung Gospel acclamations of the new Roman Catholic service can also help, as may a Gospel procession. A well-sited and attractive reading desk is also important.

A fourth reason for reading scripture springs from the role of sacred writings as witness. Scripture is read, as noted earlier, to keep the churches' life and worship alive, full and pure. To achieve this the reading must be vivid, understood and reasonably full. Preachers alone must not choose the readings as one of the latter's purposes is to correct preaching and help the rest of the church to discern God's word. Scripture is God's gift to the whole church; it is not owned by part of the Church, nor even by the preacher. It is by its public reading that scripture exercises an influence over the language and ideas used in worship.[1] This reason for Bible reading means that translations must be accurate, and raises questions about the use of paraphrases. It is again a fairly long-term function, helping to form a church's mind and imagination.

A fifth reason is more practical, helping Christians to know the Bible better, and flows from a deep conviction that scripture is 'useful' (cf. 2 Tim. 3.16). Justin's account of scripture being read 'for as long as time allows' makes it fairly obvious that his fellow Christians were serious about the Bible and that they saw the eucharist as an important source of Bible knowledge. Remarks about the influence of television on attention span

[1] e.g. sitting, as in Zaire—cf. E. E. Uzukwu *Liturgy: Truly Christian, Truly African,* p.62.

[2] See my 'Eucharist, Sacrifice and Scripture' in Colin Buchanan (ed.) *Essays on Eucharistic Sacrifice* (Grove Liturgical Study no. 40, 1984).

will not wholly explain our failure here. Nor is it enough to say that before printing Christians had no other access to scripture. Hippolytus refers to early morning teaching meetings and to those who have books at home.[1] The Didascalia urges the lay Christian 'to occupy himself with the scriptures of life'.[1] Chrysostom urges his hearers to follow up his sermons in their bibles when they are at home with their families.[1] Public reading as an instrument of public knowledge is culturally alien to us, arguably even antiquated; however it is part of the purpose of the writings that make up the Bible, and it is essential to building up a corporate knowledge of scripture.

If one reason for reading the Bible in worship is to help people know it better, much current practice and even some of the principles in our lectionaries are called into question. We must certainly avoid the impression that the church thinks that public worship will be people's main encounter with scripture, an assumption that seems quite near the surface of the ASB's lectionary ('we've selected the *important* passages for you'!). Again is it really helpful to put in the hand of worshippers collections of thirteen-verse snippets, grouped round themes and bereft of any explanation of their context? Finding your way around the Bible is hard enough without giving people another version of it in a different order! As we have seen, separate collections of readings were a very late arrival on the Christian scene; even the Book of Common Prayer is not quite a precedent for the ASB as Cranmer viewed his Epistles and Gospels as almost a devotional supplement! In 1976 Synod accepted a proposal to print a version of the ASB without readings, but this was subsequently dropped.

Limits of the Lectionary
Within the developing liturgical tradition of the church there is a very clear distinction between the lectionary for festival seasons, which the season and custom soon dictated, and that for ordinary Sundays, which was for a long time determined by local interest and need. That something profound is at work here is shown in Baumstark's observation that liturgy is more conservative 'in sacred seasons of the year'.[4] The ASB lectionary ignores the distinction, subsuming every Sunday into its festival framework. (The interminable Sundays after Epiphany, with their recurring and inadequately handled theme of Revelation, are one result of this.) The Roman Catholic lectionary makes the distinction and is much the better for it. Amongst other things it allows the lectionary to have a thematic approach to parts of the year and a semi-continuous approach to others.[5]

[1] G. J. Cuming (ed.) *Hippolytus: A Text for Students* (Grove Liturgical Study 8, 1976) section 41, p.19.
[2] Sebastian Brock and Michael Vasey (eds.) *The Liturgical Portions of the Didascalia* Grove Liturgical Study 29, 1981) ch.2, p.6.
[3] St. Chrysostom *Homilies on St. Matthew* (The Nicene and Post-Nicene Fathers, Eerdmans) p.31.
[4] A. Baumstark *Comparative Liturgy* (Mowbray, 1958) p.27.
[5] The acceptance of this diversity allows the semi-continuous reading of Acts and John in the Sundays after Easter, arguably an improvement on the repeated resurrection appearances of ASB Year 1.

However neither lectionary allows any local discretion. This has the strange effect that it is not lawful to read large tracts of scripture at the church's main service. It also leaves no room for the tradition of expository sermon series that is highly (and rightly) valued in some parts of the Church of England. It has already been argued that organizing the reading of scripture is properly the subject of corporate decision making in the church and should not be left to preachers alone. Sensible freedom might be given by legislating to allow church worship planning groups to alter the set readings outside the major festivals (i.e. not including Advent and the two weeks before Easter).

Lectionaries need to be seen as complementing and stimulating the church's encounter with scripture in the rest of its life. One way of doing this would be to have alternative lectionary modules (ugh!) of, say, four weeks, possibly linked with home group and individual study material. Preferably such a Bible reading package would be planned from scratch, rather than home and private study material added on. For example a series on Jeremiah could select different portions of the prophet for public reading and for private and home group study, and also Gospels (and, perhaps, apostolic readings) to complement the Sunday reading. Another approach is that of Scripture Union which publishes a quarterly resource *Learning All Together* that sets out a number of three- to five-week units, often linked with ASB lectionary or themes. For each Sunday they provide background study of the relevant biblical material and then different suggested approaches for sermons, adult groups and different age-groups of young people. Again a congregation could study some theological, personal or social issue, or some church report, with a range of Bible passages for private and corporate use.

The last few paragraphs raise the question of how suggestions of a common lectionary are to be assessed. This writer is very committed to the search for common liturgical patterns in church life. However, talk of a common lectionary (*the* common lectionary?) seems more suspect. Partly because it leaves no freedom for local congregational life. But more fundamentally because it is the whole of scripture that is common to the church—indeed 'normative' for it—and should operate as such. This is not to deny the North American experience in which the CCT's Common Lectionary has clearly helped the important task of local ecumenism. And obviously a lectionary is better than no lectionary. Any common lectionary needs to distinguish between the claims of its festival and its ordinary provision, and to endorse very positively the responsibility and right of local congregations to order their encounter with scripture at least in ordinary time.

Another issue that may need to be explored is whether the same lectionary is appropriate to different types of congregation. The point here is not familiarity with books or public reading; the latter is alien to most parts of British culture. Congregations differ in size, homogeneity and relationship to the locality[1], and this has implications for how their liturgy works. Within this variety the general tendency in the Western

[1] cf. *Intercessions in Worship* pp.16ff.

world is that the Sunday congregation gathers people together across at least one locality and from distinct primary Christian groups. Within this pattern the sermon, like the liturgy, is an important unifying element. However an increasingly wide-spread alternative in some parts of the world occurs with Chritians meeting mainly in much more localized groups where the lives of those who gather together are more intimately bound together.[1] In such groups encounter with the scriptures is a more immediately corporate and controversial affair and any homily plays a different role.[2] Such different church patterns would require some rethinking of lectionary principles.

How the Bible works

Another relevant question is to ask *how* God addresses men through scripture and what the implications of this are for our public presentation of scripture. Somewhat arbitrarily I shall select and look at eight features of scripture.

1. The first and most obvious comment is that God does not speak in thirteen verse units without a context! This may be ideal for the effective choreography of modern worship, but in most cases such readings need a brief introduction if the congregation are to hear them.[3]

2. An obvious feature of scripture is variety. Our public reading gives little sense of this. At one time the Bible Society tried to bring this home by printing bible books separately in a format appropriate to their literary genre. While a book is being read in church it might be possible to put up a display that gave its cultural and historical background. Introductions could help a lot ('This is part of a letter written by Paul in prison; all the Christians in Philippi would have gathered to hear it.' 'Today's reading was first spoken by a prophet to Jewish exiles in a refugee camp in what is now Iraq.' 'This is part of a love poem, probably to be sung at a wedding.')

3. Closely related to the last is the occasional nature of much of scripture, itself an expression of its humanity. Although the Bible bears witness to the importance of creeds and the power of theological ideas to shape lives, much of its literature springs from God's dealings with particular individuals or groups. Most of the Epistles arise from concrete issues in particular congregations. Much of the interest of scripture comes from the human angle or vulnerability of people in crisis situations and can easily be lost in more thematic

---

[1] Sometimes called Basic or Small Christian Communities. See David Prior *The Church in the Home* (Marshalls, 1983). The Brazilian Jesuit Jao Libanio comments that middle-class people travel to find community whereas many of these communities in Brazil grew in a street.

[2] 'In their meetings they pray and sing hymns, but the one constant is always the reading of a passage from Scripture, silent reflection on it for a few minutes, the re-reading of the same passage followed by discussion on it and its application' (Fr. Simon Sirikwa in *African Cities and Christian Communities,* Margaret Peil and others) p.44).

[3] Introductions are another art to be learned. The essence is brevity, variety and aiming to help the congregation to tune in, rather than simply summarizing the reading.

treatment. Part of Galatians is Paul's passionate anger; a good reader, a good translation and a longer reading are needed to bring this out.

4. Another feature of scripture is lament. Moltmann sees this as a vital part in worship if the gospel of the resurrection is not to make worship deceptively comfortable for the content and intolerable for the troubled.[1] Scripture is, of course, full of lament—and devotes its finest literary creation to warning the godly against quick and easy answers. The power of many psalms we are embarrassed to use lies precisely here. Of all this there is little echo in our contemporary reading. Jesus is allowed to suffer and cry out when the season permits, but others never.

5. Much of the Bible is narrative and many of its authors are brilliant story tellers. Modern practice means that few stories appear apart from those of Jesus' ministry years. Will anyone again hear the story of Joseph unfold in church? John Goldingay writes of 'narrative texts as literature which opens up a world that we may enter' and comments 'A story cannot be paraphrased or summarized without losing something'.[2] One example illustrates its power:
   'Far more than any argument, it was surely the power of the Nativity Stories and their place in ritual and celebration and song that tempered [i.e. shaped] the conscience of the West to its audacious effort to wipe out the practice of abortion and infanticide. As the hold of stories over the minds and imaginations of millions upon millions of men and women recedes, it is clear that abortion and infanticide are becoming "thinkable" again as permissible practices, even good.'[3]

6. Related to the last, and often located in narrative, is scripture's treatment of potent human themes: death, conflict, longing for children, patriarchy, gender. Imagine the power in the CCT *Common Lectionary's* idea of hearing the book of Ruth read consecutively over three Sundays.

7. Scripture is not always, or exclusively, addressed to the church; this can be obscured in liturgical reading (compare ASB's post-pentecost themes). In the New Testament Luke, Acts and John are clear examples. G. Fohrer sees at least 18% of the Psalms as non-cultic. Old Testament wisdom literature addresses men and women within the broad context of their human concerns.

8. Scripture requires a response. The lady who greeted Jesus' teaching with 'Blessed is the womb that bore you and the breasts that you sucked' (Luke 11.27) may have missed his point but at least she responded. It is easy in many a service to feel that it would have been exactly the same whatever the scripture had said. There is no attempt to allow scripture to set the agenda.

[1] J. Moltmann *The Church in the Power of the Holy Spirit* (SCM, 1977) p.273.
[2] *Anvil* vol. 1, No. 3, p.264.
[3] Paul Ramsey 'Liturgy and Ethics' in *Journal of Religious Ethics* (7/2) (1979) pp.139-171.

5. IDEAS

I conclude with some more detailed applications and suggestions.

1. Awareness

Congregations need teaching and training about this part of the service. Training in ways of participating; teaching to include the shape of the calendar and lectionary in use. 'If you didn't listen to the reading, you didn't listen to God speaking.' It can help to put the next week's readings on the notice sheet, or even a brief commentary on each of the week's readings.

2. Response

The sermon is part of the response. The second position for the Penitential section in Rite A allows it to function in response to the scripture. (It might have been better before the prayers.[1]) Both prayers and the lead-in to confession can pick up references to the readings.

One frequent difficulty in Rite A is a headlong rush through the readings to the sermon. Slowing the pace by allowing a brief response to each reading could change expectations greatly. The ancient church followed each reading by a song or prayer. A short silence after each reading could be illustrated by a picture or slide, or followed by one verse of a hymn sung meditatively. Each reading could be followed by a brief *personal* response from the reader ('I learned . . .' 'I resolve . . .' 'I was glad . . .'). Notice sheets could include a blank in which to draw or write a response in the silence. Well-chosen responsorial psalms with a good refrain could aid response.[2] Care has to be taken not to swing into too familiar a praise mood. Readings and sermons would benefit if the Gospel is not read by the preacher.

3. Themes

This seems a pretty intractable issue. A measured progress through the readings with more forms of response might soften pressure on the preacher *and* the call for themes. I think fixed themes are often harmful outside festival seasons and thematic collects increase the pressure. The right to use another ASB collect should be authorized. Some of ASB's opening and post-communion sentences are too thematic or meditative and miss the opportunity to proclaim or summon; variety here is permitted but often not used.

4. Variety

Too much variety, particularly round festivals, alienates worshippers, but with care different patterns could be adopted occasionally. For four weeks a semi-continuous reading could be read from a different part of the church, and be dramatized or followed by a short sketch.[3] An Old Testament narrative could be turned into a serial for the children. Such

---

[1] See the Roman Catholic Zairean Rite in Max Thurian and Geoffrey Wainwright (ed.) Baptism and Eucharist (WCC/Eerdmans 1983) p.205.

[2] Cf. Robin Leaver, David Mann, David Parkes (eds.) *Ways of Singing the Psalms* (Collins).

[3] See, e.g., the Bible Society *Using the Bible Series* 3 and 4: *In Drama, With Visual Aids.*

ideas would depend on competent planning and on a congregation being at home with its basic liturgical pattern. Some churches have conducted separate liturgies of the word for children.

On occasions the sermon could be abandoned and the scripture allowed more freedom. In addition to the dramatic reading of extended narrative it would be possible to expose the congregation to a particular book. 'Micah speaks'. 'Paul's letter to Philippi': with interjected commentary 'I am Epaphroditus'(!) 'Protest songs': readings from the Psalms—followed by Jesus in Gethsemane as the Gospel. This writer once helped organize a dialogue between Proverbs (a wisdom school), Ecclesiastes, Job and the Wisdom of Solomon.

A more traditional idea of very great potential is extended services of readings, often in the evening and then called vigils. The Episcopal Church of the USA's *Book of Occasional Services* includes many very fine examples of these.[1]

5. Readers

Obviously a lot depends on the quality of presentation, and the common practice of a rota of readers or a last-minute search for a volunteer is not really ideal. If the practice of brief introductions were to be adopted in such a case it could be disastrous. One practice advocated and followed up in parts of the Roman Catholic church is for the Church council to draw together a team of readers who learn and work together.[2] Folk are chosen on the basis of their ability, willingness and spiritual seriousness. Another idea might be for a parish to have a small team responsible for the reading of scripture who could meet and train those who read, and also give their mind to drawing in other members of the church. They would liaise with any drama or music groups, and could look for ways of involving primary groups in the church ('The readings each Sunday this month will be read and introduced by one of the home groups on the Snowdrop estate.').

6. Training

This is obviously vital. The great advantage of setting aside a team is that they can learn together. The Roman Catholic *Training Readers* already referred to[3] follows a series of meetings in which a group learn together. Meetings consist of practice and rehearsal (e.g. reading, introducing), information (learning your way round Bible and lectionary), and Bible study (e.g. James 1.23-25).

7. Useful Material: for this see overleaf.

[1] Even one for All Hallows' Eve that begins with the witch of Endor and ends with the war in heaven of Rev. 12! It includes fine prayers.
[2] Described in the quite excellent *Training readers* (No. 5 in *Training for Community Ministries* publ. by Collins and obtainable from Fowler Wright Books Ltd., Leominster, Herefordshire, England).
[3] See note 2 above.

Useful material for a group learning together (or for an individual) would be:

Clifford Warne, Paul White and Anne Vallotton *For Reading Aloud* (Bible Society: Using the Bible Series No. 1). A very practical personal guide.

John N. W. Wijngaards (Mayhew-McCrimmon). *Reading God's Word to Others.* Roman Catholic. Again very practical. Informative. Excellent on voice production. Stimulating on linguistics and revelation (but not, in my view, always right).

The Lion Handbook to the Bible. Excellent for making sense of Bible history, finding your way around the Bible, understanding context etc.

Anglican Worship Today (ed. Colin Buchanan et. al. Collins) and *The Alternative Service Book 1980: A Commentary by the Liturgical Commission* (CIO) give a somewhat fuller but dry account of the ASB Calendar and Lectionary than this booklet. Probably more revealing is the original JLG book *Calendar and Lectionary* (Oxford, 1967) although much has been altered.

John Gunstone *Commentary on the New Lectionary* Revised edition, vols. 1 and 2 (SPCK, 1979).